Master a system to keep your content flowing clearly and concisely in all conversations: formal or informal. Significant conversations happen at insignificant times, as well as in meetings, teleconference calls, board rooms and in email.

Fast Track to Significant Conversations: Content Guide 1

BethAnn "BA" Hengen Neynaber

Increased credibility & influence

Whether it's a team meeting, an email, a board presentation or a sales presentation, create the fast track to your success when you believe all communication is significant

When you have buy-in for your product, ideas, projects, or budget expenses you are on the fast track to success with conversations and presentations. The Fast Track to Significant Conversations System is designed for you to build new relationships quickly and cement existing relationships.

Your fast track is created on teleconference calls, informal meetings, and more, now than ever before, in your email communication. Integrating these skills into your daily conversational style will keep you on the fast track and prevent you from creating your own hidden barriers to your advancement.

If you have ever read an email or walked out of a meeting thinking, "That person has no idea what negative damage he/she just did to their career", this book is for you! Don't be that guy or woman.

The Fast Track to Significant Conversations System:

- Meets the needs of all listening styles within the audience with minimal details to immediately capture their attention and interest

- Creates a foundational action statement to get the results you seek

- Provides a built in verbal punctuation system to keep your tone conversational, interesting and engaging to build your credibility and keep the audience engaged

- Builds a fluid system of moving from topic to topic easily if interrupted by a question or comment

- Brings to you a level of focus and confidence which will transcend the content and information you provide keeping you on the fast track with your conversational tone

Creating the Foundation

Creating a framework is as simple as remembering the thoughts that ran thru your mind the last time you got called into a meeting to hear a presentation:

What is this about?
Why do we have to take the time now to address it?
What's in it for me?
What will it cost me to support the idea?
Why me —why do I have to be in this meeting?

Use a series of questions to prepare your framework each and every time you prepare for a conversation. These questions will provide you clarity of thought process, very quickly.

A consistent format for confidence

Use this format – commit it to memory – keep a copy in your electronic calendar – do not advance to any other part of the presentation – until your framework is sound. You would not build a house without a solid foundation for your family – do not build a presentation without a solid foundation for your career.

Key questions to answer before you begin to draft your foundation

Who will be in the audience?

- When talking to an association, how many are really vendors in the audience?
- When talking to a technical audience, how many years of experience in the field each person is likely to have?
- When presenting budget information, how many individuals have been in the process in the past and who is the decision maker: A committee or a specific person?
- When presenting a sales call, how many are direct decision makers and how many have subtle influence on the decision?
- When introducing change to your teams, what history do they have with the company and change in general?
- When delivering a performance evaluation, what is the length of time you have been the supervisor and what experience does the person have with the review process?
- When delivering a teleconference call, what are the times zone of the audience, what language barriers which might be present and where will the individuals dial-in from: cell or land line?

What is the reason you are presenting?

To bring people up-to-speed on a project:
Keeping people on track and on deadline, building credibility

To ask for action of any kind;
More money, close a sale, delay a deadline

To implement a change;
Stop a process, start a process

To build morale:
Award recognition for sales, service or project goal completion

To coordinate and begin a project:
A fast tracker has informally identified potential leaders within each team prior to the meeting

What are the benefits to the individuals in the room of the action you are requesting?

Yes – what about me? When determining the foundation you need to think like the people in the audience. There maybe many benefits to the company and you want ensure you to bring the benefits to departmental levels or individual goals for advancement, profit, bonus or management by objective goals whenever possible.

What are the risks to individuals in the room of the action needed?

Does a cut in the training budget mean they will need to tell their people their conference attendance scheduled will not be approved? If the expenses are not cut will there be no quarterly profit budgets? If you continue on the path of progress will you miss a production deadline and lose a contract? Will you be unable to determine the results of a marketing campaign without adding the monitoring system to the server and risk losing marketing money next year?

How do the benefits out weigh the risks to move others to action or why do the risks outweigh the benefits, creating the result of no action taken?

If hiring an additional person brings the manager out of the field and into the training role the last two weeks of the quarter, perhaps it is better to wait until the first of next quarter to ensure the sales for the quarter. If the idea sounded grand when the committee began, the cost maybe equal to the benefits yet the implementation process will actually put excessive stress on the plant and it's better to wait until the slower holiday season.

Next is a simple form, with an easy format, to build a foundational process for each and every conversation you have in significant or insignificant settings.

What is the reason you are presenting or having this conversation?

Who is your audience?

What are the benefits to the individuals in the room if the action is implemented?

What are the risks to the individuals in the room if the action is implemented?

Samples of balancing the scale of weights in risks and benefits with a foundation statement:

Sample: Cutting out one shift of overtime per department will provide the extra $10,000 needed for expense control and kept us in the 6% profit range to make bonus goals —next quarter is already ahead of schedule in sales so we have been given permission to hire again.

Sample: By implementing one weekend day of overtime in the month of May, we will stop the pattern of missed manufacturing deadlines and ensure we do not risk violating the terms of our agreement with ABC Corporation.

Sample: By booting up the implementation of the server monitor, we will be able to determine web site referrals to our page and provide the concrete data needed to ensure the marketing budget yields results. We see a direct correlation to our marketing dollars and increased consumer spending, and when spending is up on the web sites we do not risk layoffs.

Sample: By understanding the core skills needed for the key accountabilities of each position in the organization, you have the first step of attracting and selecting the individuals you desire to increase your retention and depth of succession planning when hiring.

What do these foundation statements have in common?

All action-oriented: By understanding, by utilizing, by implementing, etc

All benefit-oriented: Benefits to the audience – not you

All 1-2 sentences

Create the framework of your conversation 1-3 sentences:

Ask for the action you want

Provide a summary of the benefits

Provide any time line you need

What is the reason you are presenting or having this conversation?

Who is your audience?

What are the benefits to the individuals in the room if the action is implemented?

What are the risks to the individuals in the room if the action is implemented?

Foundation Statement:

Your Pathway to Interesting Introductions

Grab the attention of the audience by engaging them in your topic —jokes or boring beginnings derail your fast track start

Solid initial first impressions can speed the connection and engagement of your audience to your **Fast Track to Significant Conversations.**

If it's a teleconference call you may contend with home offices, sometimes even dogs or children. If it's an Association meeting after work, traffic and general fatigue may bring the down the energy in the room. If it's the boardroom after many other presentations on budget review day, it demands you be even more connecting quickly without being showy or unprofessional.

Questions to Gaining Solo Focus with an Interesting Introduction

What will assist the audience or team in securing the big picture and history they need to be right in sync with you as you introduce your foundation statement?

Does the audience or team need a piece of history as to why the change is needed, such as the inability last quarter to meet the production demands?

Does the audience or team need to understand the low unemployment numbers in your market, along with competitive salaries being offered, and the need to determine the real key accountabilities of a position before another offer is extended to the wrong fit?

Does the board need the background to the results in 4th quarter of separating marketing from advertising and the cost reductions accomplished?

Do the team members need a reminder of the goals obtained thru third quarter and why the individuals being recognized have achieved stellar results even with unexpected production delays?

To create a pathway of credibility, confidence and to quickly engage your audience, use your introductory remarks to support the foundation statement you will deliver. You have buy-in for your ideas, projects, or budget expenses – you are on the fast track to success with star quality conversational magic.

Sample: Pathway Idea One: Six months ago we began to review the territory alignment: Market penetration compared to the number of sales representatives

Pathway Idea Two: Three months ago you had the opportunity to provide us competitive factors and geographic information which gave us the complete picture of each territory.

Foundation Statement: Today we will show 3 areas which will have 3 more sales team members added and why, 2 areas where managers have requested their team members cut by 2, the redistribution of sales team members in the remaining 6 territories, and how this realignment will give us the opportunity to maximize the bonus plan for you and your team.

Sample: Pathway Idea One: As we review the production flow, and look at what the jobs really do, we are finding a different set of skills in 2014 than what were required even 5 years ago.

Pathway Idea Two: We have engaged in a process of assessing what the job's top behaviors, values and skills set are and the Senior Management team are finally in align and in touch with the production positions.

Foundation Statement: We will be implementing an assessment with our selection process to decrease the time we spend interviewing undesirable candidates based on the new skills, and the goal is to increase retention as individuals perform with excellence.

Sample: Pathway Idea One:

We learned 3 months ago of a new set of regulations concerning the documentation of cash deposits exceeding $5,000.

Pathway Idea Two:

Although a group session at the national convention would be our first choice, the date puts us too far out to comply with the regulation, so we need each manager to cover the material in a local sales meeting.

Foundation Statement:

My expectation is for each team is to complete the eLearning's by September 1, have the manager address the content in the September meeting, and we will host a national conference call to address the questions which surface in your regional meetings in October to ensure consistency.

Pathway Idea One:

Pathway Idea Two:

Foundation Statement:

Time for the framework: Build on the foundation statement with clear compartments

Stop starting with the details and keep focus on the big picture questions. Save time and energy by staying solo focused on what the audience needs to know — not what you want to say.

Too much detail will guarantee roadblocks to the *fast track results* you seek. Even if you are a highly specialized professional in a unique and leading edge technical field, skip the details except in the presence of individuals whose role is to validate the data.

You are trusted and paid for the technological knowledge and accuracy. Your fast track to success, advancement and recognition is to provide the benefits of the details and /or technology, in a format which even the least technical styles in the audience can absorb and allows you to decrease your preparation time.

By organizing your compartments of information around the foundation statement – you will always have a connection to the statement for a fluid conversation. Answer the questions in the audience's mind and if you don't know…call or email one or two of them before the presentation to see what they are expecting to happen or the details they need to know.

Use the reporter's mind set:
WHO WHAT WHEN WHERE HOW
Determine the Top 3-5 for Your Audience

- Who will be involved?
- What do they need to do?
- When does it have to be done?
- How will the process work?
- Who will benefit from it?
- What are the other options?
- When will the results be in?
- How will we measure success?
- Why do we have to do it now?
- Why do we have to implement the change now?
- Who will monitor the results?
- What happens if we don't?
- When will the team give input?
- How can we be sure it's a long term solution?
- What are the benefits?
- What are the risks?
- Who are the competitors?
- Why did we choose _____ instead of _____?

Critical to your success in assisting the audience or team members to engage and retain the information you present is to provide the information in a format conducive to both analytical (direct, factual styles) and creative (image and scenario driven) minds.

Those who learn with images and pictures painted of the process will want descriptions and examples. Those who learn from statistically data and facts will want bullet points. When presented in a conversational tone, both styles will be satisfied and will retain the information you present.

You will need to refrain from diving into numerous facts and figures which support your foundation statement. You will want to raise above all the details and create the key bullet points in which the audience have and easy ability to remember. You are the expert at details – trusted and hired for your experience. You do not need to data dump details on your audience. Whether it's your passion for campaigns or your delight in analysis of statistics – give your audience buzz phrases to remember.

If it is essential people walk away with specific factual data, you need to provide a handout when they leave or electronically. Distributing material in the middle of the presentation will cut your life line to their attention.

Reassure the audience in your introduction all crucial information will be provided as they exit for their reference. You now have a significant reason for them stay engaged in your presentation – they only need to focus on you!

Foundation Statement

1. Who, what, when, where, why or how

2. Who, what, when, where, why or how

3. Who, what, when, where, why or how

4. Who, what, when, where, why or how

5. Who, what, when, where, why or how

Determine the bullets point answers and what they have in common for each question

Meet the needs of the bottom line listeners— save hours of preparation time and tell your story clearly and concisely by beginning with just the big picture points

Sample: Who makes up the committee?

One member from every territory:
John from the small business
Sara from the corporate sales
Louise from non-profit, association sales

Why these individuals were selected does not need to be explained unless a question is raised – most audience members will be glad you made the decision or will be thrilled they don't have another project on their plate.

Sample: How will we measure success?

Monthly measures will be implemented by department.
Technology will provide the hits on a weekly basis by page
Marketing will match campaign numbers to sales of past campaigns to project weekly sales

The nitty-gritty details of the steps in which technology will gather the data or that a person on workman's comp will be gathering the marketing numbers does not need to be explained. Your role is to handle the background and your *Fast Track to Significant Conversations* needs to be based on big pictures, significant information for the audience.

Determine one example for each big picture answer

Meet the needs of the creative listeners with providing one example when an image or piece of data will support or explain the bullet point phrase. If the audience needs more examples they will ask.

The magic of the Fast Track to Significant Conversations System is with just one example you can paint a vivid image - while remaining direct, clear and concise.

Sample: What happens if we don't proceed with the overtime?

Missing deadlines will jeopardize future contracts.
- Johnson's sales are increasing at the rate of 17% a quarter and we will be eliminated from future business.

  Image:Securing only 2% of the piping business anticipated from Johnson' growth would set your holiday bonus for 2015

- We risk not meeting yearly projections

  Image: With the late penalty we will incur by missing the deadlines we will absorb the 6% profit margin we have accumulated and start at zero to rebuild the profit margins

- We will take a significant hit on our marketplace reputation

  Image: When you host the booth at the national suppliers convention in Dallas this fall, we will put our energy into "how can they be sure we will make it" rather than how can we apply our new technology to advance their sales

The format above works beautifully in email. Email is not a place to vent, not a place for humor which is difficult to discern without eye contact and vocal inflection, and is not a place to overload people with detail.

A safety check to ensure clarity is to ask yourself
– what do all the answers to this question have in
common?

Benefits
Costs
Risks
Implications
People involved
Deadline Dates
Expenses
Steps of the process
Project phases
Choices
Options
Avenues
Pathways
Goals
Requirements
Criteria
Methods
Timeframes

If one of the answers does not match the pattern of the other answers
it belongs in another question compartment. Perhaps it is just part of
the detail that is not significant to contributing to the action you need
from the foundation statement.

Sample: Foundation Statement

By implementing a web based learning system we will meet the needs of consistency in policy, product and company goals to all teams and will reach the remote team members who are chronically left out of the more informal communication which occurs in the local offices. This is imperative with our expansion of services to new markets which do not justify a sales office or local management and does not increase our travel expenses or time involved by management.

Compartment: What is the anticipated time frame in which the system can be functional?

Bullet One: The time line begins with receiving the final bids, which are due June 1.

One Image or Example: We have reviewed 10 systems and we narrowed it down to 3. We then secured references and actually had direct access to designed modules and had the opportunity to have "hands-on" learning experiences. One system was superior with the ability to have interactive quizzes of the information to validate comprehension of the materials.

Bullet Two: Part two of the timeline occurred simultaneously as the training team surveyed the field for needs.

One Image or Example: 10 topics rose to the surface consistently from both the operational and sales sides of the business. Customer service policy was number across the board from both teams for clarity of the policies and procedures of returning product to the warehouse. The team then submitted the current written policies to the senior management of customer service, the warehouse and accounting to review what is written and what is reality.

Bullet Three: Part three of the timeline is final approval.

One Image or Example: With two steps of the timeline completed, we are awaiting the final bid from our preferred vendor and we have every indication it will come in within the anticipated budget. With final approval to purchase given today, we will meet our goal of having the system functional for the field by first part of third quarter.

Sample: Foundation Statement

In reviewing the survey results of the sales team concerning the amenities provided at the national convention, we can decrease expenses by 10% from last year's convention and still have a dynamic, inspirational meeting of top notch caliber.

Compartment: What did the sales team tell us this survey?

Bullet One: The welcome gift with the company logo is not appreciated.
One Image or Example: Comments included the fact that they win the company trinkets in sales contests or they already have the item we provide them, such as a CD holder. Many suggested they would prefer a raffle with one large prize, perhaps even donated by vendors. The cost savings would be significant – 300 gifts at approximately $25 each or $10,000 when shipping and custom work is included.

Bullet Two: Another consistent suggestion was one free night instead of two planned activity nights.
One Image or Example: The next set of comments concerned the second event night, which runs in the ballpark of $40,000. By providing dinner and simple refreshments such as a coffee bar or dessert bar by the pool, we would honor their request to socialize with team members they rarely see, and the side note mentioned was some of them would get more rest to be more alert in the sessions by not having an activity, and then socializing.

Bullet Three: The rest of the comments were diverse, yet the strongest comments came from the management to provide drink tickets to each person rather than an open bar before dinner.

One Image or Example: I believe we are all in agreement with less alcohol and the company's increased mission of healthy living. Although there will still be individuals who indulge excessively, managers believe those who don't will increase when the additional alcohol beyond two drinks is at their personal expense. The savings anticipated is $10,000 for the two nights.

Sample: Foundation Statement

You have been with us for 6 months John and you have become a knowledgeable team member in our products and services. We are here today to address concrete actions I need to see implemented in order for you to make the next 6 month goals for your sales quota and how to implement all the knowledge you have gained for you to enjoy the commission structure available to grow your income.

Compartment: What kind of performance improvement is expected from you John?

Bullet One: John, you close 10 sales per week but the volume billing potential of the sales is running 25% behind your goal.

One Image or Example: To assist you in identifying larger target sales, you will submit your anticipated prospecting firm names to me on Friday by noon so I can review and we can discuss if they have the potential you need in our one-on-one session.

Bullet Two: Simultaneously, you need to enhance the activation rate of the accounts you are signing contracts with by 10%.

One Image or Example: John, your accounts are slow to begin and some never begin. Other team members are running 98% activation of the accounts sold and you are running 88%. Sometimes this happens when individuals do not feel comfortable making the switch due to insufficient training. I will come with you on two calls next week to review your training style and information provided at closing.

Bullet Three: The paperwork issue of timely expense reports is going to become imperative to you receiving compensation for your expenses. New policy requires all mileage and receipts to be submitted within 15 calendar days of the end of the month.

One Image or Example: You have been running 21 to 37 days in submitting your expense reports. Let's talk about how we can improve your organizational system or assistance you need in time management to ensure you receive compensation for your expenses.

Preparing for the question with bullet points and one example

Continue to meet the needs of the bottom line listeners and the creative listeners in the same format as you prepared your compartments

Answering questions with a Fast Track pattern

It is easy and simple to remember:

1) Repeat
2) Pause
3) Use one bullet point with one image or example

It does not matter how many people are present, someone is drifting. Nothing is more frustrating than an answer being provided when someone missed part of the question. You also take control of the question by repeating a portion of it for clarity.

Sample:

Audience: Why do we need to decrease expense for the convention if the budget has been approved?

Repeating the question: The need to decrease expenses has come from Senior Management's desire to ensure the convention is a staple of our training program.

Pause and breathe

By showing we have a quality convention in content, without the frills of items not really appreciated by the sales team, we show our dedication to delivering exactly what is needed to improve morale and keep the team current on policy and product.

Sample:

Audience: How do you expect us to find time to do these benchmarks with our current work load?

Repeating the questions: Finding the time to participate in a benchmark will be well worth the scheduling commitment and the benefits of decreasing the time in interviewing and training will enhance your schedule.

Pause and breathe

Each one of you will likely be asked to participate in two benchmarks. We will be much attuned to the production needs and one option we have is to replace one staff meeting a month with the benchmark process. As we clarify the positions, we will be able to only refer top candidates to you for the interview process and once the benchmarking is complete, we will not need the time investment going forward.

Sample:

Audience: How do you plan to provide the new benefits plan via electronic media when people have so many individual questions?

Repeating the question: Electronic media will be just one of the ways we present the new benefit package.

Pause and breathe

The fundamentals of a benefit package via an electronic media have been proven to be very successful because individuals can listen to specific modules which they have a concern with more than once. The organizations we've reviewed have a 3 phase approach. First are the general modules electronically. Next is a team meeting with a Human Resource Representative addressing the most common questions. Finally, individuals will be able to call our team with specific questions, just as they have been able to do in the past.

The Next Step:

You are polishing and refining your content. The organization of your content will provide you automatic improvements in your delivery if your content is fluid and in increments you can retain without memorizing mounds of information.

Presence is the ability to maintain your personal style and conversational tone, even when the opinions of the audience differ when it comes to the next action you need for results.

Fast Track to Significant Conversations 2: Developing Your Presence will provide you the skills and tools to have a relaxed body language, a strong, clear voice and the polish to take your career to the next level as you build rapport with your audience.

What is the reason you are presenting or having this conversation?

Who is your audience?

What are the benefits to the individuals in the room if the action is implemented?

What are the risks to the individuals in the room if the action is implemented?

Foundation Statement:

What is the reason you are presenting or having this conversation?

Who is your audience?

What are the benefits to the individuals in the room if the action is implemented?

What are the risks to the individuals in the room if the action is implemented?

Foundation Statement:

What is the reason you are presenting or having this conversation?

Who is your audience?

What are the benefits to the individuals in the room if the action is implemented?

What are the risks to the individuals in the room if the action is implemented?

Foundation Statement:

What is the reason you are presenting or having this conversation?

Who is your audience?

What are the benefits to the individuals in the room if the action is implemented?

What are the risks to the individuals in the room if the action is implemented?

Foundation Statement:

What is the reason you are presenting or having this conversation?

Who is your audience?

What are the benefits to the individuals in the room if the action is implemented?

What are the risks to the individuals in the room if the action is implemented?

Foundation Statement:

Pathway Idea One:

Pathway Idea Two:

Foundation Statement:

Pathway Idea One:

Pathway Idea Two:

Foundation Statement:

Pathway Idea One:

Pathway Idea Two:

Foundation Statement:

Pathway Idea One:

Pathway Idea Two:

Foundation Statement:

Pathway Idea One:

Pathway Idea Two:

Foundation Statement:

Pathway Idea One:

Pathway Idea Two:

Foundation Statement:

Foundation Statement

1. Who, what, when, where, why or how

2. Who, what, when, where, why or how

3. Who, what, when, where, why or how

4. Who, what, when, where, why or how

5. Who, what, when, where, why or how

Foundation Statement

1. Who, what, when, where, why or how

2. Who, what, when, where, why or how

3. Who, what, when, where, why or how

4. Who, what, when, where, why or how

5. Who, what, when, where, why or how

Foundation Statement

1. Who, what, when, where, why or how

2. Who, what, when, where, why or how

3. Who, what, when, where, why or how

4. Who, what, when, where, why or how

5. Who, what, when, where, why or how

Foundation Statement

1. Who, what, when, where, why or how

2. Who, what, when, where, why or how

3. Who, what, when, where, why or how

4. Who, what, when, where, why or how

5. Who, what, when, where, why or how

Foundation Statement

1. Who, what, when, where, why or how

2. Who, what, when, where, why or how

3. Who, what, when, where, why or how

4. Who, what, when, where, why or how

5. Who, what, when, where, why or how

Foundation Statement

1. Who, what, when, where, why or how

2. Who, what, when, where, why or how

3. Who, what, when, where, why or how

4. Who, what, when, where, why or how

5. Who, what, when, where, why or how

BethAnn brings to you experience in "real world settings":

- Manager of Sales Training and Development for Wells Fargo Merchant Services
- Director of Training and Development for Optum (A UnitedHealthcare Company)
- Coach and Trainer for Executive Speaking, Inc.
- Direct Market Entry, Defending Market Sales Coordinator, National Sales and Area General Management in the Credit Reporting Industry
- Business owner of Solutions Unlimited Communications and Gap Training Solutions
- International seminar leader, key note speaker and private coach to hundreds of companies and non-profit organizations

Send her an email at elizabethneynaber@yahoo.com and receive the second step to your development FREE:

Guide 2 – Fast Track to Significant Conversations Presence

Develop your vocal style, your physical presence and your pace to match your new content skills.

BethAnn's Presentation Seminars and Private Coaching include video-taped feedback to enable fast-paced, immediate improvements in your style in a safe and encouraging experience.